**Crafty
Inventions**

suoᴉʇuǝʌuI
ʎʇɟɒɹƆ

**Crafty
Inventions**

**Crafty
Inventions**

suoᴉʇuǝʌuI
ʎʇɟɒɹƆ

Crafty
Inventions

suoitnevnI
ytfarC

Crafty
Inventions

Crafty
Inventions

suoitnevnI
ytfarC

WEAPONS AND WAR

by Gerry Bailey

illustrated by
Steve Boulter and Jan Smith

Reading Adviser:
Susan Kesselring, M.A., Literacy Educator
Rosemount-Apple Valley-Eagan
(Minnesota) School District

PICTURE WINDOW BOOKS
www.picturewindowbooks.com

First American edition published in 2005 by
Picture Window Books
5115 Excelsior Boulevard
Suite 232
Minneapolis, MN 55416
877-845-8392
www.picturewindowbooks.com

Publisher: Felicia Law
Design director: Tracy Carrington
Project manager: Karen Foster
Author: Gerry Bailey
Editors: Rosalind Beckman, Christianne Jones,
   Jackie Wolfe
Designed by: Jacqueline Palmer, assisted by
   Simon Brewster, Will Webster, Tracy Davies

Cartoon illustrations: Steve Boulter (Advocate)
Make-and-do: Jan Smith
Model-maker: Tim Draper
Photo studio: Steve Lumb
Photo research: Diana Morris
Scanning: Imagewrite
Digital workflow: Edward MacDermott

Library of Congress Cataloging-in-Publication Data
Bailey, Gerry.
Weapons and war / written by Gerry Bailey ; illustrated
by Steve Boulter and Jan Smith.
p. cm. — (Crafty inventions)
Includes bibliographical references and index.
ISBN 1-4048-1048-X (hardcover)
1. Military weapons—Popular works. I. Title. II. Series.

U800.B25 2005
623.4—dc22   2004024422

Crafty Inventions

WEAPONS AND WAR

Table of Contents

What Weaponry Can I Use?

Early people have been using some of their tools as weapons. A stout rod or a club is more effective than bare fists. A battle-axe is even better. Now people want a more efficient weapon. Perhaps using a stronger material would help.

Bled's people have had a hard time lately. Whenever it's time to do some hunting or crop planting, along comes another tribe with more men, more clubs, and more battle-axes.

When faced with trouble, Bled realizes it's best to keep his distance, so his tribe usually dives for cover into the nearest woods.

If only I had powerful weapons to defend my land from invaders.

Now Bled has found a fertile piece of land with great hunting nearby. He doesn't want his people to move yet again. If he tries to defend his land, though, they may lose everything—including their lives.

WHAT CAN HE DO?

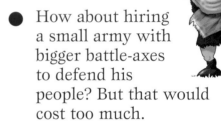

- How about hiring a small army with bigger battle-axes to defend his people? But that would cost too much.

- Perhaps he could give each of his men an extra digging stick to defend themselves. Oh well, maybe not ...

- Using bronze knives might help. But they're too short—his men would need to get dangerously close to the hatchet men.

- If he made extra-long knives, his men could fight out of reach of the axes. Great idea, but the knives keep breaking. The bronze just isn't hard enough for long blades.

I know! I'll use that new metal I've heard about. It's a bronze made of tin and copper, which is much harder than the usual bronze made of copper and arsenic. My extra-long knives will be killer blades!

Bronze made of copper and tin created a whole new armory of stronger and sharper weapons, including the sword.

Sharp blade

A **sword** is a weapon that is used in hand-to-hand combat, either to stab or to cut. A typical sword is made up of a blade and a handle, called a **hilt**. The blade may have one cutting edge or two, depending on its design. Early swords were made of bronze, but by 1000 B.C. they were made of iron, which was much harder and could be made sharper.

There are many different shapes and sizes of sword. The Romans used a **gladius**, a short sword about 22 inches (55 centimeters) in length, with a plain, practical hilt. A Scottish claymore is a two-handed sword, with a long, very broad blade, while a Persian **shamir**, or scimitar, is curved. The Japanese Samurai sword has a tough, very sharp, curved blade, and an ornate hilt.

Metal

Metals such as copper and tin are found anywhere in Earth's crust, but they can only be mined if they are formed into long, thin deposits called veins.

Veins form when continents collide and push Earth's crust down into the hot center of Earth where they melt. Lighter granite rocks then rise back into the crust to form large globules called plutons. These rocks solidify, or harden, very slowly. Those materials with the lowest melting point, such as metals, harden last. So the metal seeps up into the surrounding hardened rock, where it finally cools and solidifies into veins. When these veins are pushed close to the surface of Earth, they can be mined. Early people learned how to mine and work metals about 8,000 years ago, probably in the Near East.

POISONOUS METAL

Copper mining used to be a dangerous job, as miners were exposed to toxic gases. Metal-workers used to add the poison arsenic to copper to make the metal easier to work with, which made it even more toxic. In Roman mythology, the the blacksmith god, Vulcan, was often pictured as a sick and ugly person. Perhaps he was affected by the poisonous fumes from in his forge ...

Metal is found in veins in Earth's crust. Using a powerful drill, the miner is able to reach the metal deep inside the rock.

Inventor's words

gladius
hilt
pluton
shamir
solidify
sword
vein

Make a Persian scimitar

You will need

- marker pen
- foam board or thick cardboard • craft knife or scissors
- craft glue • string
- double-sided sticky tape
- large plastic milk container
- stapler and staples
- paints and brush

1 Draw a sword shape on the foam board or on layers of cardboard stuck together with glue, as shown. Cut out.

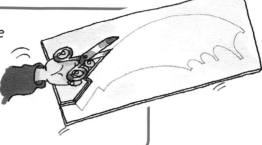

2 Glue on extra pieces of cardboard to strengthen the handle and round off the grip.

3 Cover the handle in double-sided tape, and wrap string around it.

4 Cut off the top of a plastic milk container. Slide the sword handle through the spout and attach another piece of board to the base, as shown. Staple together.

5 Now paint and decorate your sword.

How Can I Make a Better Bow?

Soldiers have been using the bow and arrow as a weapon of war for centuries. But it's not so useful anymore, as it's difficult to fire an arrow through the new chain mail armor. And when in range to shoot, soldiers are also more likely to be shot at.

Edwin's been a yeoman soldier for years. He's always off fighting in some war or other. Mostly, he fights against the Welsh and the Scots. He doesn't mind hand-to-hand combat because he's big and strong. He also has a huge staff and a very sharp sword. His favorite weapon, though, is a bow.

The problem is that when Edwin's close enough to shoot, he's also in danger from enemy arrows. Even worse, his simple bow isn't all that effective against knights in armor.

I'll have to improve my bow, or it will be the death of me!

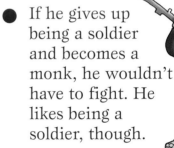

WHAT CAN HE DO?

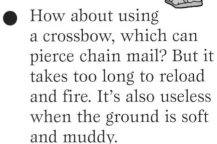

- If he gives up being a soldier and becomes a monk, he wouldn't have to fight. He likes being a soldier, though.

- How about using a crossbow, which can pierce chain mail? But it takes too long to reload and fire. It's also useless when the ground is soft and muddy.

- Perhaps he could make a quick-firing crossbow. But even when firing more quickly, it's still too slow. A simple bow is faster.

- Only a conventional straight bow can shoot really fast. He has to make a bigger, lighter bow out of some special material. But what can he use?

I need a sturdy wood that will bend well. Tough, elastic wood from a yew tree should work. I'll make an extra-long longbow out of yew wood. Then I'll be able to shoot more arrows than a crossbow—and from a greater distance.

In the Middle Ages, archers could shoot up to 20 arrows a minute, from a distance of about 907 feet (275 meters).

Extra-long bows

Military longbows were as high as the archer, while the arrows he shot were half his height. Longbows could let a more powerful arrow fly over a greater distance, which revolutionized the way large-scale combat was conducted. They were first used effectively at the Battle of Crécy, in northern France, in 1346. French soldiers were cut to pieces, and knights were forced to dismount and fight on foot, becoming easy targets. The longbow was usually made of yew, although elm was sometimes substituted. It took 99 pounds (45 kilograms) of pressure to pull the great bow, so archers needed strong muscles, especially in their back.

Elasticity

Elasticity describes how a material bends. An **elastic**, or flexible, material can bend without breaking. Paper and polyethylene, for example, are very elastic. A rod of iron is not.

Materials are sometimes gauged by their **elastic limit**. This is the maximum force from which an elastic object will return to its original shape. If a force greater than this limit is applied, the material will become permanently bent. Materials bend because of **stress**, or the force put on them. How much a material bends or changes shape is measured as **strain**. And the amount of strain a material shows is called its **elastic modulus**. If the elastic modulus of a longbow was too high, it could not be bent. If the elastic modulus was too low, the longbow would bend too much and have very little power.

Inventor's words

elastic
elastic limit
elastic modulus
elasticity
longbow
strain
stress

Modern composite bows have a high elastic modulus. Arrows shot from today's bows can reach distances of over 2,541 feet (770 meters).

Make a bow and arrow

You will need

- craft knife and scissors
- 3.3 ft (1 m)-long thick bamboo stems
- double-sided tape
- string • white cardboard
- stapler and staples
- smaller thin bamboo stems
- craft glue • feathers
- paints and brush

1 Cut a notch into both ends of the 3.3 ft (1 m) bamboo. Wrap each end in sticky tape, then wrap the tape with string.

2 Cut a length of string that is shorter than the bamboo. Tie a loop at each end. String the bow with a loop held in each notch.

3 Wrap the center of the bow with sticky tape. Then wind string around the tape to make a handle.

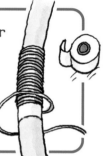

4 Cut out two arrowhead shapes from cardboard. Place them on either side of a small bamboo rod and staple and glue together. Wrap string around sticky tape just below the arrowheads.

5 Glue feather pieces on to the tail sections. Use tape and string to complete. Cut a notch into the very end of each arrow to fit the bow string. Paint and decorate.

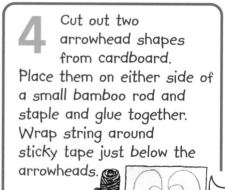

11

How Can I Protect Myself in Battle?

Fighting between great landowners is getting worse by the day. Armorers are making sharper, more accurate weapons, and a knight's chain mail armor no longer offers real protection. Knights are especially at risk when they're riding on horseback.

Sir Pomfrit is helping out his lord, Baron Fitzherbert. He's leading about 50 stout men in battle, but he's worried that that he is not well protected.

Sir Pomfrit only has his old suit of chain mail covered with a wool tunic to protect him. A well-placed shot from a crossbow could pierce the chain mail and kill him on the spot.

Sir Pomfrit always rides into battle. Recently, he was nearly dragged off his favorite mare, Dumpling, and a lance almost pierced the chain mail joint near his neck. Phew, that was a narrow escape!

Help! These crossbow bolts and lances are coming thick and fast.

WHAT CAN HE DO?

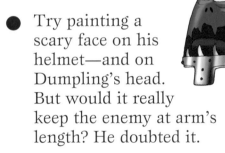

- Try painting a scary face on his helmet—and on Dumpling's head. But would it really keep the enemy at arm's length? He doubted it.

- How about adding pieces of iron to his chain mail? Sounds like a painstaking task ...

- Perhaps a suit made of iron would help. He could get a blacksmith to make one. Hmm, it'd be rather heavy, though.

- Steel would be lighter. A pair of steel trousers and a steel shirt to go with his steel helmet would be great. But he'd still the problem of how to move with all that metal.

12

I've got it—metal plates are the answer! Instead of a solid suit, I'll make plates of steel shaped to my body. Then I'll fasten them together with leather at the joints. I'll be protected by steel, but it won't cramp my fighting style.

Plate armor protected knights—and their horses—when they fought battles or jousted.

Heavy armor

Plate armor was developed in Europe during the 14th century, because **chain mail** armor, made up of tiny rings of metal linked together ... could be pierced by crossbow arrows or crushed by maces. Plate armor consisted of large pieces of steel that covered the entire body. The suit, worn by a knight, included a helmet, breastplate, gauntlets or "gloves," and shoes called sollerets.

Even the knight's horse wore plate armor. Although it offered good protection, plate armor was heavy, hot, and very expensive. Later, it was decorated for fashionable parades and tournaments, and was sometimes etched or gilded with silver or gold. But even plate armor could not protect against the new gunpowder weapons; by the late 16th century, plate armor went out of use.

Steel

An alloy is a mixture of one metal with a small amount of other metals. Steel is an alloy made from iron that is mixed with a small amount of carbon. It can be made much harder and stronger than iron and is also easier to shape. A special kind of steel called stainless steel is made by adding chromium. Stainless steel does not corrode, which means it does not rust.

At first, steel could only be made by heating wrought iron, iron beaten with a hammer, with flux, a material that helped the metal burn. This was done in an air tight container, allowing the metal to melt without combining with oxygen. But only about 99 lbs (45 kg) could be made at a time, making it very expensive to produce. Then, in 1856, Henry Bessemer invented a process, which involved blowing air through the mass of molten metal, that made steel more affordable.

ARTISTIC ARMOR

The finest ornate armor was called Gothic armor, which was made in southern Germany and northern Italy. It was more attractive than the original bulky plate armor. Sometimes, the armor was fluted, or grooved, for style and extra strength.

Molten metal can be poured into a mold and left to cool until it sets into a solid shape.

Inventor's words

alloy
chain mail
flux
plate armor
steel
wrought iron

14

Make a plumed Roman helmet

You will need

- felt tip-pen • large balloon
- strips of newspaper
- craft glue • scissors
- cardboard • string • feathers
- double-sided sticky tape
- thin cardboard • thin wire
- stapler and staples
- paints and brush

1 Draw a helmet shape on a balloon, and cover with layers of newspaper soaked in a solution of half glue, half water. When dry, pop the balloon.

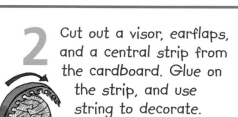

2 Cut out a visor, earflaps, and a central strip from the cardboard. Glue on the strip, and use string to decorate.

3 Roll up some feathers in a strip of cardboard covered with sticky tape. Decorate the base with string.

4 To assemble the helmet, tape cardboard hinges to the earflaps. Make holes at the side of the helmet, thread wire through the hinges and helmet, and twist together on the inside. Staple on the visor.

5 Stick on the plume, then paint your helmet.

How Can We Shoot Accurately?

Gunpowder is being used to fire cannonballs, which can easily destroy castle walls. Smaller firearms, which can be held by one soldier, use the same sort of mechanism, but they're not accurate. Soldiers miss their targets too often. Wouldn't it be great to have a small, accurate weapon?

Warfare is changing now that gunpowder is in use, and small firearms are available. A round bullet can pierce body armor.

A blunderbuss can fire a handful of shots so that some pieces have a good chance of hitting the target. A musket also makes a handy club.

Missed again! Will our bullets ever reach their target?

Musketeers are feared by the enemy—except when they are over 100 paces away. Then they are more likely to miss their target.

A musket ball does not travel far in a straight line.

WHAT CAN THEY DO?

- A lengthier gun barrel might keep the bullet moving straighter for longer. But the gun would be too awkward to aim and fire.

- How about putting some kind of stabilizing device on the bullet— like the feathers on an arrow? The explosion would probably blow them off!

- Making the bullets and the gun barrel very smooth might do the trick. No such luck—it has the opposite effect.

- They could design a bullet that's shaped to make it spiral. A spiralling object flies through the air in a straight line.

Aha! Making the bullet spin will work, but first we need to alter the barrel. If we cut spiral grooves in the barrel, it'll make the bullet spin as it shoots out. The spin should keep it moving in a straight line.

Rifles were more accurate than muskets—but much longer. Some were 6 ft (2 m) in length.

Spiral groove

A **rifle** is a type of firearm. The inside of its barrel, or muzzle, is **rifled**—it has a spiral groove running from back to front. This spiral groove causes a bullet to spin as it is fired. This makes the bullet travel further and in a straighter path through the air. The first rifles were made in Italy and Germany, probably in the late 15th century.

The Jaeger rifle, used in central and northern Europe, was the first really accurate rifle. It was developed around 1665. German immigrants brought the Jaeger to America, where it was modified. It had a longer barrel and was even more accurate. It became known as the Kentucky rifle, from which many modern rifles developed.

Gyro effect

When a top spins, it turns around an imaginary line that runs through its center from top to bottom. Once the top is spinning, it is very hard to make it change its position. This is true of any spinning object and is called gyroscopic inertia. Because of gyroscopic inertia, Earth remains in the same position, spinning on its axis as it orbits the Sun. The north end of the axis always points toward the North Star.

A gyroscope is an instrument that uses gyroscopic inertia. It is made up of a spinning wheel and an axle joined to supports called gimbals. When the wheel spins, it stays in the same position no matter how the supports move. It can be used in a special kind of ship's compass called a gyrocompass. A gyrocompass always points north, no matter how the ship moves. A rifled firearm makes a bullet spin around its axis. The spinning bullet travels in a fixed direction because of gyroscopic inertia.

A human gyroscope can be great fun—but it needs a trained operator to start and stop spinning!

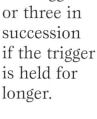

Q: Is a musket or a rifle more accurate?

A: A rifle.

Q: What motion helps a bullet travel further and in a straighter path?

A: Its spin.

Q: In which direction does a gyrocompass always point?

A: North.

How Can I Shoot Automatically?

Infantry men have been using rifles to shoot at the enemy from a distance. They are faster to load than muzzle loaders but can only fire as quickly as a soldier can pull a trigger. If a firearm could fire automatically, its user would have a real advantage.

Hiram knows that in wars such as the American Civil War, most soldiers carry a rifle of some sort. But soldiers fight in groups and need to get close to the enemy. This makes them easy targets, especially when they have to stop and reload their rifles.

If a soldier could avoid reloading, he'd be safer. He'd also be able to fire more bullets at the enemy. A gun that reloads and fires automatically is the answer.

In the 1860s, Richard Gatling's weapon came close, but it wasn't fully automatic.

It's about time we had a fully automatic gun that fires and loads itself!

WHAT CAN HE DO?

- What if he duplicated the Gatling gun, which uses a crank, or lever, and tried to make it more efficient?

- Or see if there is a quicker way to load the belt of cartridges into the gun.

- How about finding some way to power the cycle of loading, firing, and ejecting the cartridge that does not involve a mechanical lever action.

- Perhaps he should look at the only other power source involved in firing the gun—the explosion of the cartridge itself ...

When the cartridge explodes, gas expands and creates a force in all directions. The forward force pushes the bullet out. I'll use the backward force of the gas to operate a mechanism to throw out the old cartridge and load a new one.

Invented by Hiram Maxim in 1883, the first machine guns had the firepower of about 80 rifles.

Rapid fire

A **machine gun** is a small, rapid-firing, automatic gun that fires cartridges one after another. It was used to devastating effect during the World War I, 1914-1918. A modern machine gun can fire between 400 and 1600 rounds of ammunition each minute. A machine gun barrel ranges from .22 caliber to 20mm.

Ammunition is fed into it by a cloth or metal belt, or from a cartridge holder called a **magazine**. Automatic machine guns fire so rapidly that they become very hot. They have to be cooled by water or air. Large machine guns are heavy, so they are mounted on a support. Others are light enough to be hand-held.

Hot gas

When a substance such as gunpowder is ignited, or set on fire, it burns very fast and produces a hot gas that expands, or grows, outward. The rapid expansion of the gas produces a burst of energy and noise called an explosion.

If the gas is confined in a small space, it cannot expand, which causes great pressure. The pressure is equal in all directions. If the expansion takes place in a space with an opening at one end, such as the barrel of a gun, the pressure can be used to push a bullet out of the barrel at high speed. A rifle bullet can reach over 2,970 ft (900 m) per second when it exits the muzzle of the gun. A machine gun uses the explosion and expansion of hot gas to power the firing cycle as well as to fire the bullets. The backwards pressure against the cartridge case is used to eject it, cock the firing mechanism, and move a new cartridge into the firing chamber, which is now ready for the cycle to begin again.

SYNCHRONIZED FIRING

The first airplanes with machine guns had a major problem—the bullets often struck the propeller. In 1915, Dutch engineer, Anthony Fokker found the solution. He designed a device to synchronize the firing sequence of the gun with the rotation of the propeller. This way the stream of bullets hit their target—not the propeller.

Machine guns mounted on the top of tanks can swivel around in all directions.

Inventor's words

expand
explode
ignite
machine gun
magazine

Make a bamboo machine gun

You will need
- bamboo stems • craft glue
- rubber bands
- wire coat hangers
- string • wire cutters
- craft knife • foam board
- double-sided sticky tape
- thin wire • cardboard
- plastic pot
- popsicle sticks
- paint and brush

1 Position two pieces of bamboo stem in an A-shape. Push bamboo struts in between the long bamboo stems, as shown. Hold in place with glue and elastic bands. Twist coat hanger wire around the pointed end to make a hook, and secure with string.

2 From the foam board, cut a large cog to fit in the rear gap of the gun. Make a hole in the center with a piece of bamboo, and glue in place. Use string and tape to hold wire handles at either end of the bamboo.

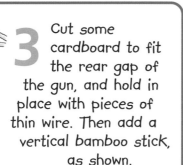

3 Cut some cardboard to fit the rear gap of the gun, and hold in place with pieces of thin wire. Then add a vertical bamboo stick, as shown.

4 Cut a diagonal slot into each side of the cardboard housing, as shown. Slide up the firing cog and secure with a piece of cardboard and sticky tape.

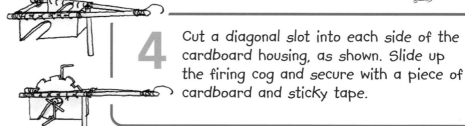

5 Decorate a plastic pot with painted popsicle sticks. Stick the foot of the gun into the upturned pot. Put a rubber band around the wire hook and onto a cog-tooth, and wind backwards. Repeat until 6-8 bands are loaded. Wind slowly forwards to 'shoot' the bands.

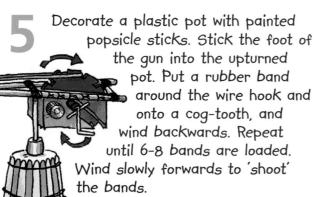

How Can I Make a Big Bang?

Soldiers are discovering how to use gunpowder in hand guns such as blunderbusses. These new weapons are great because they can pierce armor, but they only strike down a single enemy. Soldiers would cause a lot more damage if they could make a bigger explosion.

Jethro is tired of having to load his flintlock every time he fires a shot. It's time-consuming and dangerous. And while he loads, someone is shooting at him! Sometimes, he thinks he might as well set fire to his powder horn and throw that at the enemy!

How can I take a potshot at the enemy without *blowing* myself up at the same time?

He'd have to throw it mighty quickly, though, or he'd *blow* himself up. He could put in a fuse wire to delay the explosion, but it might fall out as he throws it. Still, the idea has promise.

WHAT DID THEY DO?

- The Chinese had made an exploding weapon as early as 1220. They attached a fuse to it and threw it at the enemy.

- To make the device even more devastating, they filled it with pieces of metal as well as gunpowder.

- Around 1400, soldiers in Europe began to use similar weapons, but they were not particularly reliable.

- By the 1600s, some soldiers were specially trained to use a weapon called a grenade, named after the French word for pomegranate. But the fuse system was still hit and miss. Or rather, more miss than hit!

I know! Instead of a fuse we'll add a pin, which can be pulled out, and a timing device. When I pull the pin, the timing device will give me a few seconds to throw the grenade before it explodes. Here goes ...

Today, most infantry soldiers carry grenades as part of their arsenal of weapons.

Mini explosive

A **grenade** is a small, hollow explosive weapon that is thrown at an enemy or fired from a special gun. There are several different types of grenades. **Fragmentation** grenades contain a coil of wire that has notches in it. When the grenade explodes, the wire shatters. Chemical grenades are filled with either gas, smoke, or white **phosphorus**.

Phosphorus is a substance that burns quickly with a very smoky fire. Illuminating grenades are used at night or in the dark for lighting up enemy positions so that soldiers can see their objectives more easily. Some grenades are fired from hand-held rocket launchers. These are known as rocket propelled grenades, or **RPGs**.

Fragmentation

Fragmentation means broken into small pieces. In weaponry, it refers to types of bombs or shells that break up when they hit their target. They are used against troops, road vehicles such as trucks, and aircraft that are still on the ground.

A fragmentation bomb is made up of a heavy metal case that breaks up into thousands of pieces when it explodes. Some fragmentation bombs also contain metal bars that break into jagged pieces on impact. Fragmentation shells fired from artillery guns have special fuses that are set before the shell is fired. The fuse is timed so that the shell explodes just above the heads of enemy troops. A **cluster bomb** is another type of fragmentation weapon. Hundreds of small bombs are packed into a container. After it has been dropped, the container opens, scattering the tiny bombs over a wide area.

Cluster bombs are particularly unpopular because they often fall into civilian areas.

GRENADE COCKTAIL

During World War II, 1939-1945, when Finnish soldiers couldn't get ordinary grenades to throw at their Russian enemies, they made their own. They stuffed flammable, or burnable, liquid, such as petrol, into a glass bottle, and used a piece of cloth as a fuse. The device was called a Molotov cocktail, after the Soviet Foreign Minister, Vyacheslav Molotov—whom they hated.

Inventor's words

cluster bomb
fragmentation
grenade
phosphorus
RPG

Make a grenade pencil holder

You will need

- thick cardboard
- glass jar
- double-sided sticky tape
- cardboard • toilet paper
- craft glue
- plastic bottle top
- hammer and nails
- thin wire • bamboo
- circle of plastic
- paints and paintbrush

1 Wrap cardboard around the jar and tape. Add a few extra strips of cardboard around the middle, as shown.

2 Soak toilet paper in a mix of craft glue and water. Shape cubes from the pulp and stick them on to the jar. Make the cubes bigger around the middle. Leave to dry.

3 To make the lid, cut off the top of a plastic bottle. Push this into the top of the jar. Ask an adult to help you punch 2 small holes in the bottle lid and the bottle neck with a nail. Thread the lid to the neck with wire, as shown.

4 Repeat step 3 on the front of the lid. But instead of joining the wires, shape 4 loops, as shown.

5 Push a piece of cane through the loops and fix a circle of plastic to one end as a ring-pull for the grenade. Paint and decorate.

How Can We Move Heavy Weapons?

Until World War I, big guns such as cannons were carried on wagons pulled by horses. There was a limit to how much the horses could pull though, and sometimes the gun wagons got bogged down in mud.

In 1912, an Australian engineer named Lancelot de Mole sent plans for a tracked fighting vehicle to the British War Office. His plans were similar to the "landships" that the military had been thinking about creating. But the War Office didn't act upon the idea.

We sure need a strong vehicle that can carry heavy weapons and move over rough ground easily.

Nothing was done until there was a stalemate in the fighting on the Western Front in 1914. Infantry were being cut down by machine guns. The army needed an armored vehicle with guns that could advance on the enemy, safe from fire.

WHAT DID THEY DO?

- Colonel Ernest Swinton suggested using a version of Holt Caterpillar tractors, used to tow guns across country. Idea not taken up.

- Captain Murray Sauter thought a bigger version of the armored cars used in Belgium might work.

- Winston Churchill, first Lord of the Admiralty, set up a Landship Committee. It built a prototype vehicle, using Bullock commercial track units.

- Lengthened tracks were used to build the first vehicle, "Little Willie." But it was top-heavy and the tracks weren't long enough to clear enemy trenches.

Let's build a new tank with a lower body and longer tracks. The front wheels will be bigger than the back ones. The amount of track in contact with the ground will be as much as a 39.6 ft (12 m) diameter wheel. Now that'll give a firm grip!

The first tank, nicknamed "Mother" or "Big Willie," had a top speed of 3.72 mph (6 kph).

Armored vehicle

A **tank** is an armored fighting vehicle that runs on **caterpillar tracks**. It can carry arms such as machine guns, rockets, flame throwers, or even nuclear weapons. Tanks were invented during the World War I, although Leonardo da Vinci had drawn designs for them in the 15th century. The first tanks, in action in 1916, used tractor engines.

These were difficult to maneuver and needed several men to work the controls and change gears. Modern tanks use powerful diesel engines. They have a four-person crew consisting of a driver, a gunner, a loader, and a commander. Today, tanks are the most important land-fighting vehicles, able to withstand heavy bombardment.

Ballistics

Ballistics is the branch of engineering that studies how bullets, shells, missiles, and other objects behave and move when they are fired from a gun or launcher. There are three types.

Interior ballistics deals with the way an object moves as it travels down the barrel of a gun. Engineers study how weight and speed affect its flight, as well as how it slides down the barrel.

Exterior ballistics is concerned with what happens when an object leaves the barrel. Engineers look at the effects of gravity, air, and the speed of the object. Gravity pulls the object toward Earth, for instance, while air resistance slows it down.

Terminal ballistics looks at what happens when the object hits its target. Engineers examine the damage, which depends on the make-up of the target and the object fired. Damage can be caused in many different ways, from impact and blast to radiation or biological harm.

SHORT TURN

A tank is steered differently from a car, whose wheels turn from left to right. Instead, the tank driver applies the brakes to one track, while skidding the other. This allows the tank to turn completely around on its own length.

Today's largest tanks are an army's most heavily armored vehicles.

Inventor's words

ballistics
caterpillar tracks
exterior ballistics
interior ballistics
tank
terminal

Make your own tank

You will need

- scissors or craft knife
- cereal box
- double-sided sticky tape
- thick cardboard • small boxes
- craft glue • plastic tub
- thin cardboard dowels
- pen cap barrel
- foil cake pan
- corrugated cardboard
- paints and brush

1 Cut in and push down one side of the cereal box and attach with double-sided sticky tape.

2 Add small bits of cardboard for decoration, then glue small boxes at the front and rear.

3 Glue a plastic tub on to a cardboard circle. Push a piece of dowel through the tub to make a gun turret with a pen cap barrel. Stick a foil cake pan on top.

4 Push a short dowel through the bottom of the turret. Now push the turret into the tank body, and add an antenna.

5 Cut out four track faces. Decorate two with wheel shapes.

6 Cut out track strips from corrugated cardboard. Line with double-sided tape and attach to the track faces.

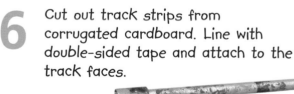

7 Attach tracks to tank, and paint.

How Can I Sink a Ship?

Sea battles have been taking place since ships first sailed the seas. Since the 16th century, sailors have been using cannons, sometimes row upon row of them. It takes many cannon-balls to sink an enemy ship. If only a ship could be hit below the waterline in a surprise attack.

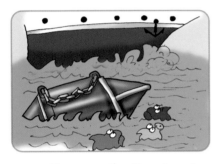

Sometimes a floating bomb called a torpedo was used to try to sink enemy ships. The torpedo was launched into the water and left.

With luck, an enemy ship would run into it. The explosion could break its hull and sink the ship. But it didn't happen very often.

Another method was to attach the torpedo to a pole and ram another ship. But that didn't work very well, either. Then Austrian navy captain Giovanni Luppis took a plan to a Scottish engineer named Robert Whitehead.

I need help with my plan for a self-propelled torpedo.

WHAT DID HE DO?

- Luppis had to think of a way for the torpedo to propel itself. Somehow, the torpedo had to find its own way to the target.

- This meant using some kind of engine or propelling system that fits into, or onto, the torpedo itself.

- A streamlined tube shape was the most efficient shape because it's aerodynamic. This meant the propelling system had to be inside the torpedo.

- A steam engine would be no good under the water. But Robert Whitehead had a better idea. What if he were to use something as simple as air?

Of course!
Compressed air is the answer.
A compressed air pack in the torpedo will create the power to push it along. When one end of the pack is opened, a push equal to the push of the escaping air will power the torpedo forward.

Preparing a torpedo for action on a German U-boat.

Explosive warhead

A **torpedo** is a weapon used to sink enemy ships. It is made up of an explosive warhead in its nose, an engine, and a tail with rudders and propellers. Some torpedoes carry nuclear warheads. Torpedoes can be fired by surface ships, but they are often more effective when fired from submarines.

A torpedo is fired underwater toward the hull of an enemy ship. When it reaches its target, the warhead explodes. Modern torpedoes can be launched by rocket boosters and sometimes contain electronic guidance systems that steer it toward its target. The torpedo was invented by Robert Whitehead in 1867.

33

Pushing force

The great scientist Isaac Newton studied motion, or movement. He wrote down a number of laws that govern movement so we can understand it better. His third law states that for every action there is an equal and opposite reaction. It's this law that explains why rockets go up and why early torpedoes sped toward their targets.

Early torpedoes used a container of compressed air, or air pressed very tightly into a space smaller than it would normally occupy, to power them forward. If a hole or opening is made at one end of the container, the air, which is under great pressure from being compressed, rushes out. This is the action. At the same time, a pressure equal to that of the air rushing out creates a push that hurls the container in the opposite direction. This push powers the whole torpedo forward as the air rushes out of the opening at the back.

Torpedo fire caused terrible damage during World War II.

BLAST OFF!

Rockets work in a similar way to torpedoes. The fuel and oxygen mix is burned to make hot gas under pressure. The gas flowing from the rear of the rocket is the action. The reaction is the thrust that pushes the rocket up.

Inventor's words

action
compressed
motion
reaction
torpedo

Make your own model torpedoes

You will need

- scissors or craft knife
- large cardboard box
- cardboard • acetate • plastic bottle • craft glue • gravel
- thin cardboard tubing
- styrofoam block
- skewer sticks • cellophane or food wrap • strong wire
- double-sided sticky tape
- marker pen • foam board
- paints and brush

1 Cut one side of the box, and lift up the top flap. Strengthen the flap with cardboard backing, and then tape acetate across the top of the side walls.

2 Cut off the end of the plastic bottle at an angle. Place inside the box, and glue it to the side to make a submarine hull. Glue the base of the box and sprinkle with gravel to make the seabed.

3 Cut a torpedo out of cardboard tubing. Make a rounded tip out of styrofoam and plug at one end. Push a stick through the tube and styrofoam, and glue a cardboard propeller to the end. Add a cellophane trail. Repeat for the second torpedo.

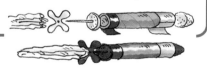

4 Push two wires up through the base of the box, and tape in place. Push wires into the torpedoes.

5 Draw and cut out a boat shape from the foam board, as shown. Make a hole in its hull. Slit the acetate and slot into the sinking ship. Glue crumpled food wrap around the ship for a watery effect. Paint your torpedoes.

How Do I Control a Missile?

Ever since William Congreve developed a simple rocket-powered missile in the 1800s, soldiers have been eager to improve on his design. Some unguided missiles were used in the World War I, but they were only used to shoot down military balloons.

During World War II, Germany tried, unsuccessfully, to bomb Great Britain into defeat.

But German bombers were being shot down regularly. It wasn't worth the cost of sending them at all. What could they do?

What we need is a guided missile to protect our pilots and aircraft.

The German leaders decided that another form of attack must be developed. They thought that sending unmanned craft was the way forward. But what kind?

WHAT DID THEY DO?

- German scientists were ordered to look at rocket and jet engine technology to get ideas for powering an unmanned craft.

- A top secret research base was built on the island of Peenemunde in the Baltic Sea.

- Scientists built a pilotless aircraft, named the V1, which was powered by a jet engine. It used a ground-based guidance system.

- The V1 was used to bomb London after the Allied invasion of France, but it wasn't accurate enough to be used against the southern ports, where supplies were sent from.

Rocket power has to be the answer—a rocket with a preset guidance system that travels at 3,286 miles (5,300 km) per hour. Once launched, the guidance system will direct the rocket to its target, where the explosive warhead will detonate.

V2 rockets flew very high and could hardly be heard as they approached their target.

Finding its way

A **guided missile** is a vehicle that carries an explosive warhead and is directed to its target by a guidance system. It can be fired from ground to air, from ground to ground, from air to air, or air to ground. Guided missiles are powered by rocket engines, although jet engines are sometimes used. Some guided missiles are self-propelled.

They have a computer and other guidance equipment on board. Others are controlled from the ground. Operators guide them by radio from a control center. Most guided missiles are shaped like a rocket, using small fins at the back for changing direction. The largest are around 59.4 ft (18 m) long and can carry a nuclear warhead.

Radar

Radar is a way of finding the position of objects. A radar set sends out radio waves. These bounce off, or are reflected back from, objects. The bounced waves cause a bleep on the receiving screen of the radar set. A map outline on the screen shows where the object is located.

Some very advanced guided missiles use a type of radar called phased-array radar to guide them to a target. The system has a transmitter and receiver of waves at ground control, and a radar antenna in the missile. When the radar detects a target, the computer predicts its direction and decides when to launch the missile. The radar then tracks the target and the missile. When the missile homes in, its radar picks up bounced waves from the target and transmits them to control. Data from control and from the missile itself guide the missile in closer, until the fusing system triggers the warhead.

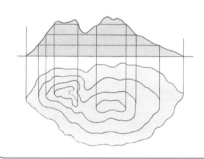
Radar-controlled missiles are used against fighter planes and other missiles.

Inventor's words

guided missile
phased-array
radar
receiver
transmitter

38

Make a rocket-launcher

You will need

- hammer and nails
- 12 in (30 cm) long piece of wood
- string • rubber bands
- cardboard • dowels
- clothespin • paper towel tube
- craft knife and scissors
- small cardboard boxes
- paints and brush

1 Ask a grown-up to help you nail two pieces of wood together to make a T-shape. Attach a rubber band to each end of the T-bar.

2 Make a hole at each end of an oblong piece of cardboard. Feed through the rubber bands through the holes, and push a short piece of a dowel through each loop, as shown.

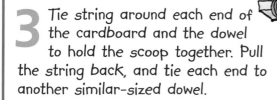

3 Tie string around each end of the cardboard and the dowel to hold the scoop together. Pull the string back, and tie each end to another similar-sized dowel.

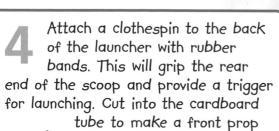

4 Attach a clothespin to the back of the launcher with rubber bands. This will grip the rear end of the scoop and provide a trigger for launching. Cut into the cardboard tube to make a front prop for the launcher.

5 Make missiles from small cardboard boxes. Paint and decorate.

How Can We Finally End the War?

The Chinese made the first bombs in the 13th century. Then in 1845, the Austrian army attached bombs to balloons. During World War I, bombs were dropped from planes. Even larger bombs were built during World War II, but now the Allies need something far more powerful.

During World War II, the German air force dropped 2,200 lbs of bombs on many European cities. The destruction was terrible.

Meanwhile, in the Pacific Ocean, the Japanese air force bombed American ships at Pearl Harbor on the island of Hawaii on December 7, 1941.

In the last years of the war, the Allied air forces retaliated, bombing and destroying German towns. But the war in the Pacific continued. Perhaps one mighty bomb might end it.

Now, what kind of bomb might be more explosive than any other?

WHAT DID THEY DO?

- The United States government was advised by scientist Albert Einstein to develop a weapon that gets its energy from splitting atomic particles.

- Scientists studied uranium, a radioactive element that gives off energy when it is broken down. Dangerous stuff!

- The Manhattan Project was set up. Scientists made plutonium and built an atomic reactor with 45 tons of uranium.

- They created the first artificial atomic chain reaction, in which the nuclei, or centers, of atoms are split. Result? A HUGE blast!

Let's pack a bomb with a rod of uranium or plutonium. A small explosion as the bomb hits its target will begin an atomic chain reaction. The explosion of energy will be far larger than any bomb ever used before.

The damage done by the first atomic bomb was greater than anyone anticipated.

Atomic energy

An **atomic bomb** uses the energy created by **nuclear fission**, which occurs when atoms are split. Only three kinds of atoms can be used for nuclear fission: two types of **uranium** atom and a type of **plutonium** atom. If the mass of uranium or plutonium, called the **critical mass**, is great enough, fission will start off a chain reaction where more and more atoms are split.

This causes a nuclear explosion. An atomic bomb is activated by a conventional explosion. To create a critical mass, the bomb either compresses, or squeezes, an amount of material into a smaller mass, or shoots one amount into another. This starts off the chain reaction and causes a violent nuclear explosion. The first atomic bombs were used against Japan in 1945.

Nuclear fission

Nuclear fission takes place when the nucleus of an atom splits. Heavy radioactive elements—an element is a solid, liquid, or gas that is made up of just one type of atom—such as uranium, split into new elements and release nuclear energy.

An atom is made up of a number of negatively-charged electrons that move around a nucleus. A nucleus contains protons, which have a positive charge, and neutrons, which have no charge at all. When a single neutron particle on its own is made to hit the nucleus of an atom of uranium or plutonium, the nucleus splits. This turns a small amount of matter into a large amount of energy. The split atom releases more neutrons that split more atoms in a chain reaction. The energy produced can be used for different things, including the making of electricity.

Atomic energy can be used to power engines as well as for making bombs. But it can still be very dangerous if it isn't treated with great care.

NUCLEAR FUSION

Nuclear fusion is the opposite of nuclear fission. Nuclear fusion happens when two atoms fuse, or join together, at very high temperatures. Light elements such as hydrogen fuse to make new elements and release nuclear energy. A hydrogen bomb uses fusion to create a violent explosion.

Inventor's words

atomic bomb
critical mass
electron • neutron
nuclear fission
nucleus
plutonium
proton
uranium

Q: When did the Japanese bomb Pearl Harbor?

A: December 7, 1941.

Q: Who advised the United States to develop a weapon that got its energy from splitting atomic particles?

A: Albert Einstein.

Q: What creates the energy in an atomic bomb?

A: Nuclear fission.

Glossary

Action In Newton's third law of movement, an action is a movement in a particular direction that causes an equal reaction, or movement, in the opposite direction.

Alloy Solid substance made by melting a metal and then mixing it with smaller amounts of metals or non-metals. Afterward, the mixture is cooled until it becomes solid again.

Atomic bomb Weapon that uses the energy created by atomic fission.

Ballistics Branch of engineering that studies how bullets, shells, missiles, and other objects behave and move when they are fired from a gun or launcher.

Caterpillar tracks Band of linked steel plates that pass over wheels on each side of a tank.

Chain mail Armor made from interlaced metal rings. It was in use between 1000 and 1400.

Cluster bomb Bomb that is made up of thousands of smaller bombs that spread and explode as it hits the ground. Many international organizations want to ban the use of cluster bombs.

Compressed Pressed tightly together.

Critical mass Mass, or quantity of matter, of uranium or plutonium needed to cause an atomic explosion by fission.

Elastic Material that returns to its original shape after being bent. It can mean flexible, or easily bent.

Elastic limit Maximum force from which an elastic object will return to its original shape. If a force is applied greater than this limit, the material will become permanently bent.

Elastic modulus Amount of strain a material shows when it is bent.

Elasticity Ease with which a material can return to its original shape after being bent.

Electron Tiny speck of matter that is usually part of an atom. An electron moves in orbit around the nucleus of an atom.

Expand Become bigger or take up more space. Most gases, liquids, and solids expand when they are heated.

Explode Expand very quickly, creating a huge amount of energy.

Exterior ballistics Branch of ballistics that studies what happens when an object such as a bullet or shell leaves the barrel of a gun.

Flux Substance that is mixed with a metal to help it burn.

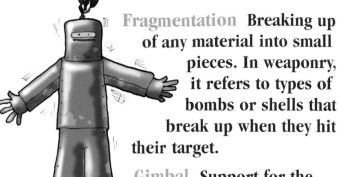

Fragmentation Breaking up of any material into small pieces. In weaponry, it refers to types of bombs or shells that break up when they hit their target.

Gimbal Support for the wheel-and-axle part of a gyroscope.

Gladius Short sword with a plain, practical hilt used by Roman soldiers.

Grenade Small bomb thrown by hand.

Guided missile Vehicle that carries an explosive warhead and is led to its target by a guidance system.

Gyrocompass Special ship's compass that always points north, no matter how the ship moves.

Gyroscope Instrument that uses gyroscopic inertia. It is made up of a spinning wheel and an axle joined to supports called gimbals. When the wheel spins, it stays in the same position no matter how the supports move.

Gyroscopic inertia Tendency of a spinning object to maintain its position as it turns around its axis.

Hilt Handle of a sword or dagger.

Ignite Set on fire.

Interior ballistics Branch of ballistics that studies what happens to an object such as a bullet or shell inside the barrel of a gun.

Longbow Extra long bow made of yew wood used by English bowmen during the 13th and 14th centuries.

Machine gun Small, rapid-firing, automatic gun that shoots cartridges one after another.

Magazine Cartridge holder that feeds ammunition into a machine gun or quick-firing rifle.

Motion Movement of a body in a particular direction.

Neutron Tiny particle of matter found at the nucleus of an atom. A neutron has no electrical charge.

Nuclear fission When the nucleus of an atom is split, releasing huge amounts of energy.

Nucleus Center of an atom, containing protons and neutrons.

Phased array Special type of radar used to guide missiles to a target. This kind of radar shifts its beam electronically rather than mechanically. The shift can be made instantly, so it is much quicker.

Phosphorus An object is phosphorus when it is coated with phosphors, solids that give out light when hit by electrons.

Plate armor Heavy armor made up of solid plates of steel.

Pluton Globule of rock that has solidified beneath Earth's crust.

Plutonium Chemical element made from uranium. It is a silver, radioactive metal.

Proton Tiny particle of matter found in the nucleus of an atom. A proton has a positive electric charge.

Radar Electronic device that sends out pulses of radio waves. Some waves are reflected by objects such as planes and ships back to the radar device, which can then calculate where the objects are.

Reaction Opposite and equal force to the force caused by an action.

Receiver Electronic device used to pick up radio waves, or signals, from the atmosphere and change them into sound or pictures.

Rifle Type of firearm. The inside of its barrel, or muzzle, is rifled; it has a spiral groove running from back to front. The spiral groove makes a bullet spin as it is fired.

Rifled In weaponry, the spiral groove running the length of the barrel of a firearm.

RPG Rocket-propelled grenade.

Shamir Type of scimitar, or sword, with a curved blade.

Solidify Become solid.

Steel Alloy made from iron and a small amount of carbon. It may also contain silicon, nickel, or chromium.

Strain Amount a material bends or changes shape.

Stress Force put on materials to make them bend or change shape.

Sword Weapon with a sharp edge or edges. It is used in hand-to-hand combat either to stab or to cut.

Tank Armored fighting vehicle that runs on caterpillar tracks. It can carry arms such as machine guns, rockets, flame-throwers, or even nuclear weapons.

Terminal ballistics Branch of ballistics that studies what happens when a bullet hits a target.

Torpedo Weapon used to sink enemy ships. It is made up of an explosive warhead, an engine, and a tail with rudders and propellers.

Transmitter Electronic device connected to an antenna that transmits radio waves.

Uranium Radioactive element. It is a heavy, white-colored metal.

Vein Crack in rock that is filled with ore.

Wrought iron Soft iron made by continually reheating and hammering pig iron. Wrought iron is used for making tools, weapons, screws, and nails.

Index

Tools and Materials

Almost all of the materials in this book can be found around the house or bought at your local art or craft shop. If you cannot find the exact item, try to replace it with something similar.

Most of the models will stick fast with craft glue or even wallpaper paste. However, some materials need a stronger glue, so be careful when using these as they may damage your clothes and even your skin. Ask an adult to help you.

Always protect furniture with newspaper or a large cloth, and cover your clothes by wearing a work apron.

User Care

Take special care when handling sharp tools such as scissors, pointed gadgets, pieces of wire, or craft knives. Ask an adult to help you when you need to use them.